AF349059

Early Life Leadership in the Classroom

Resources, Tidbits & Strategies to Grow Great Leaders

CHRISTINA DEMARA

Early Life Leadership in the Classroom: *Resources, Tidbits & Strategies to Grow Great Leaders*
Christina DeMara

Published by DeMara-Kirby & Associates, LLC
P.O. Box 720335 McAllen, Texas 78504

Disclaimer:
Early Life Leadership in the Classroom: Strategies, Tidbits, & Resources to Grow Great Leaders is based on the research, professional opinion, and experiences of the author, and it does not promise anything to the reader.

CHRISTINA DEMARA
LIFE · LEARNING · LEADERSHIP

Early Life Leadership Books & Resources

Early Life Leadership in Children
101 Strategies to Grow Great Leaders

Early Life Leadership
101 Conversation Starters and Writing Prompts

Early Life Leadership Workbook
101 Strategies to Grow Great Leaders

Early Life Leadership Workbook for Girls
101 Strategies to Grow Great Leaders

Early Life Leadership Kids Journal

Early Life Leadership in the Classroom
Resources, Strategies & Tidbits to Grow Great Leaders

Author's Notes

Read & Believe

"I want the children in my life to grow up to be strong, ethical leaders!" -Christina DeMara

Open Heart & Open Mind

First and foremost, we must accept each child as a possible leader, with a unique personality. Children must be respected as formulated thinkers, imaginative creators, self-motivated doers, and effective leaders with embraced strengths and weaknesses, regardless of labels and stereotypes. The purpose of this book is to equip adults with the tools to speak life and leadership into our children.

Early Life Leadership Infusion Defined

"Early Life Leadership Infusion is the act of instilling, teaching, modeling, guiding, and developing leadership skills and concepts in children."

—from Early Life Leadership in Children
by Christina DeMara

A Note from the Author

Dear Valued Reader,

Early Life Leadership in the Classroom is a short introduction to leadership for children. It is an impactful starting point for any classroom, home, church, community center, doctor's office, or counseling center.

After the 2017 U.S. presidential election, I found myself, as many of you did, wondering how the United States could only come up with a few candidates. These few candidates came with questionable backgrounds and experiences. This generated a host of internal questions on leadership for me. For example, where do leaders come from, and what qualifies someone to be a leader?

My in-depth research on leadership stems from the lack of and the need for better leaders for a better tomorrow. All my research pointed to the question, how do we grow and cultivate ethical leaders? Growing ethical leaders starts with you. As an educator, mother, and leader, I wrote this book to help bring awareness to a huge problem we face, the lack of leadership development in children.

We understand the urgency there is to help

nurture our children for a better tomorrow. Their tomorrow is so much more different than the present we now face. We need to build stronger communities, better municipal infrastructures, and stronger schools in order to have stronger leaders and a stronger future. This free eBook is my way of bringing awareness and contributing to the solution for this ongoing problem.

I hope that this book ignites your thinking and changes the way you love and teach the children in your life. Because gone are the days where "little red school learning" will be enough. Colleges and today's workforce are seeking leaders. That is why I developed Early Life Leadership books and resources. But bigger than all of that, students need to know and understand leadership in order to be all that they are destined to be.

With warm wishes and a heart of gratitude,

Christina DeMara
christinademara@gmail.com

Contents

Teaching children leadership skills can help children:

» Improve social skills.

» Build relationships.

» Boost their self-esteem.

» Understand conflict resolution.

» Improve speaking, communication and problem- solving skills later in life.

» Identify their strengths and weaknesses.

» Work and understand different personalities and cultural backgrounds.

» Develop leadership skills for future leadership opportunities.

» Work with others successfully.

What Is Early Life Leadership Infusion?

Early Life Leadership Infusion is the act of instilling, teaching, modeling, guiding, and developing leadership skills and concepts in children.

After children are born, we quickly condition them. We start establishing their conditioning with feeding and sleeping patterns. We condition them to walk, play, and learn home and social norms. Why should leadership be any different? There is nothing wrong or selfish in wanting your child to be a strong, humble, and effective leader.

All children are capable of learning leadership concepts. However, they will all learn at different paces, and for some, leadership might be harder to learn than for others, but it is possible if you believe and are intentional!

This little book was designed to help teachers infuse and bring leadership into the classroom.

There are different ways to infuse leadership concepts in a child, such as modeling, discussion, and real-life experiences. This book is important because it consists of leadership activities and discussion prompts, and these things are the glue that helps leadership concepts stick to the child.

8 Best Practices for Teaching Children Leadership Skills

One of the most frequent questions I get asked by teachers is, "With all the content demands, how do I teach children leadership skills?" You don't need to have a leadership degree or be in a leadership role to teach your students leadership skills. In this section, there are eight different teaching principles that will help you teach leadership skills to children.

Clear Objective

Make sure the intent of the leadership skill you want learned is clear. Be intentional and precise with your words. Visuals are also an excellent way to help with understanding.

EXAMPLE OBJECTIVE

Honesty: Leaders tell the truth, even if it means they might be in trouble.

Action: The student will show an understanding of honesty through role-playing and group discussions.

DISCUSSION PROMPT:

Honesty is important because:	When I am honest with others, I am:

Honesty is difficult because:	When you are honest with others, you must take their feelings into consideration because:

Child-Centered Activities

Concentrate on what the child is doing when developing activities for children. Yes, you need to be involved, but you should be guiding with open-ended questions and facilitating.

Activities I Have Tried	Activities I Want to Try
1.	1.
2.	
Outcome	2.
1.	
2.	3.

Example of Classroom Activities

» Leadership Book Corner in Your Classroom

» Leadership Cards (at the back of the book)

» Leadership Read Aloud to Students

» Leadership Role Playing and Modeling

» Leadership Family Tree Completed
at Home to Share with Classmates

» Meet the Leader:

• Bring leaders in from the community to speak to students.

Modeling

Modeling is a very effective strategy for teaching. Some concepts are very abstract for children, but when we show them ourselves through our actions, the pieces start to come together. In the classroom, I often model leadership skills by scaffolding my actions, "I Do," "We Do," and "You Do." This helps build mastery.

Example 1

"I Do" (Adult) Models apologizing.
"We Do" (Adult & Child) Adult and child apologize to each other.
"You Do" (Child) Children apologize to each other.

"I Do"

"We Do"

"You Do"

Notes

Example 2

"I Do" (Adult) Models delegating.
"We Do" (Adult & Child) Adult and child delegate to each other.
"You Do" (Child) Children delegate to each other.

<table>
<tr><td>"I Do"

</td></tr>
<tr><td>"We Do"

</td></tr>
<tr><td>"You Do"

</td></tr>
<tr><td>Notes

</td></tr>
</table>

Example 3

"I Do" (Adult) Models asking for help from team members. ("Team, I need ideas for how to plan for parent night?")
"We Do" (Adult & Child) Adult and child ask each other for help.
"You Do" (Child) Children ask each other for help.

"I Do"

"We Do"

"You Do"

Notes

Example of Leadership Modeling Statements:

"I bumped into Jack, and I am going to apologize because that's what leaders do."

"I am going to let everyone have a chance to play with the ball because leaders don't leave anyone out."

"I'm upset with Jack this morning, but I am ready to shake his hand and be friends because leaders forgive people. We all make mistakes.."

"I am going to listen to everyone's ideas because good leaders listen."

"I need to watch what I say because leaders don't put people down."

10 Leadership Skills Adults Need to Model for Children

1. Being slow to anger
2. Giving others sincere praise
3. Holding yourself accountable
4. Looking others in the eye when shaking hands
5. Addressing a situation that is wrong
6. Giving others constructive feedback
7. Exploring and respecting different cultures
8. Resiliency and how to work through difficulties
9. How to work with and understand different personalities types
10. Knowing the gifts and strengths of others

Relevancy

Kids love to ask, "Why?" And that's okay. Tell them why. Always explain how events and lessons connect to their everyday lives. "Because I said so" does not work anymore. Children want to know how an activity is connected to their lives. Please encourage learning by explaining how and why. Encourage them to give you examples from their lives. This may be done through class discussions.

Example of Relevancy:

» Use an example of the student's personal items or people they know in their own lives.

» Ask them to bring in a picture or item from home.

Mix It Up

Students learn in different ways (visual, auditory, hands-on, and through reading and writing). A child's learning can be effectively supported using multiple teaching techniques and styles of instruction.

Examples of Mixing It Up:

» Videos

» Hands-on projects

» Journals

» Having students bring something from home to share

» Presentations.

What visual representations can I use?

What can we explore or research together?

How can make a small impact in the
classroom, school, or community?

What can we learn by creating with our hands?

How can asking questions help us learn more?

Positive Reinforcement

Children want to please. They crave feedback and attention. Using intentional feedback is an excellent way to move children in the right direction.

Examples of Positive Reinforcement:

"Sara, I loved the way you took the initiative by taking the trash out. You are a great leader!"

"Sam, I really like the way you said please and thank you. Those are things I like to hear! You are a great example and leader!"

Concrete Concepts

Real examples are things we use to teach the child in our everyday environments. For example, if you are going to teach counting, the lessons for a rural family might be very different from those used by a family living in a city. One family might count chicks, and another might count cars passing by.

Other examples to demonstrate concrete concepts are pictures and family mementos (souvenirs, shells, rocks, snow globes, postcards). As a teacher, I once passed out brown lunch bags to my students before they went home and asked them to bring something to school that starts with the letter we were studying. The next morning the kids came in with their bags.

We all sat on the carpet in a circle and shared. The letter for the week was *P*. One child brought a pen. The second child brought a picture of her grandfather she called Papa, and another child brought a piece of bread she called pan. These children all brought in concrete objects that they connected with when seeing the letter P, and because they all had different backgrounds, they all brought something different.

Examples of Concrete Concepts:

» Bring something to share with the class that leaders use or need.

» Bring something to class that represents leadership.

» Who are the leaders in your family? Bring a picture to class to share their story.

» What book or historical figure represents leadership to you?

» What do to you want to be when you grow up and who are the leaders in that field?

8
Student Teaching

Have students teach the class. Teaching what you have learned to someone else represents the mastery of a concept. Understanding occurs when children are encouraged to take responsibility for their learning because they are more deeply involved in higher-order thinking, analysis, and evaluation.

Examples of Student Teaching:

Group 1. Teach about the importance of trusting others.

Group 2. Teach about the importance of giving the whole team credit.

Group 3. Teach about the importance of learning leadership through history.

10 Early Life Leadership Skills Children Need to Know

Leaders Set Personal Growth Goals

Talking about and reflecting on one's own future in leadership is a great thing! Personal growth occurs when we set goals, learn, read, or explore something we want to make better in ourselves. Encourage students to set personal goals.

Why is this important? As leaders, we never stop growing and learning. Starting this habit of setting leadership goals at an early age is essential. In the classroom, all students are a work in progress. Leadership is an area where we are all continually growing.

How do I teach this? Guide students through the thought process. Have them ask themselves open-ended questions, such as "Where do I want to lead and why?"; "Where am I going and how am I going to get there?"; and "What can I do to be a better leader in school?" Students can set one personal or class leadership goal, so you all can grow together and discuss your experiences.

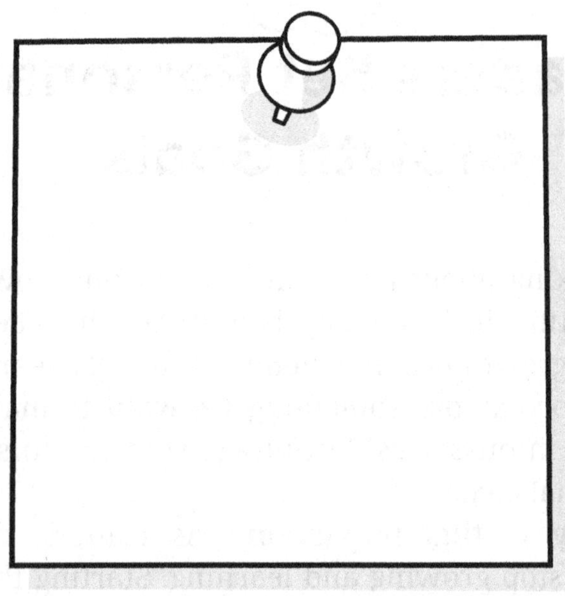

Leaders Understand Loyalty

When you are loyal, you are committed to a person or goal. This is good leadership and socialization skills.

Why is this important? Loyalty creates trust, respect, and unity. Not only is it important to be loyal to people, but you also need to be loyal to your goals and dreams. Loyalty is the key to maintaining long friendships and accomplishing your goals.

How do I teach this? Talk about what it means to "be loyal to those who are loyal to you." Through group discussion or drawing, have students discuss or illustrate the answers to the following questions:

What does your loyalty look like? Maybe you are loyal to your family, church, team, coach, or childhood friends.

Who are the people who are loyal to you? Will they help you when you need it?

Are they there for you when you are feeling down? Are you loyal to them?

3

Leaders Respect Differences

Leaders respect differences in ideas, gender, race, disability, and religion.

Respect is deserved by everyone, and it fosters an appreciation for diversity and a positive environment. Students need to learn this as early as possible because we are all different like fingerprints.

Why is this important? Leaders set the example. It is crucial that leaders respect differences. This encourages others to do the same thing. We do not have to agree with everything, but we need to respect differences and treat everyone in our school with respect. Respect is not only a classroom skill but a very important life skill. This may be incorporated with citizenship in the classroom.

How do I teach this? Instead of simply disagreeing with someone, get to know people with different ideas, genders, races, disabilities, and religions. Look for their strengths and good qualities. The best thing for adults to do is model and talk about the differences when you see there is a lack of understanding. There are also diverse books that are fun to read and offer information on whatever deeper understanding the student may need.

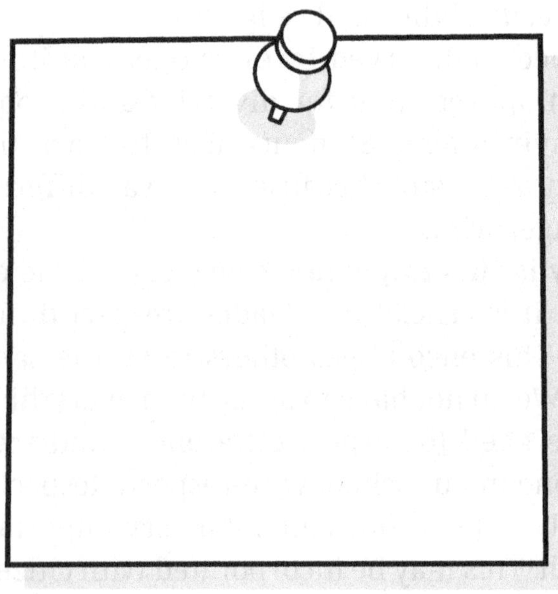

Leaders Still Have Fun

If you take everything seriously, you will miss the goodness of life. Good leaders understand the importance of having fun.

Why is this important? Having fun is important for your brain and your heart. Having fun ignites creativity and builds morale among teachers and students in the classroom. Laughing and feeling good may help reduce stress and helps with the emotional well-being of both the teacher and students.

How do I teach this? Take time to play with your class. Disconnect from technology and go outside and play! Talk about fun with your students! What is it and what does it look like? This will give you deeper insight into your students' minds and imaginations.

Leaders Can Say "I'm Sorry"

Leaders understand that apologizing when they should is a strength, not a weakness.

Why is this important? Apologizing is important because it is the right thing to do. Great leaders understand that apologizing shows maturity, increases respect, increases trust, and is one of life's most important leadership and life skills.

How do I teach this? There are three ways you can teach a child to apologize:

» Role-play using real-life experiences.

» Take time to talk about what "I'm sorry" looks like and why it's important.

» Model by apologizing to students when necessary.

6

Leaders Build Negotiation Skills

Every good leader knows the art of compromise. Negotiating doesn't mean someone wins and someone loses. It means we both walk away feeling decisions were fair for both.

Why is this important? Teach students negotiation skills like never giving in without asking for something else in return, for example, "Let's make a deal." As leaders, we want everyone to feel like they won. This skill is essential for students to learn because as leaders, we want to leave situations where both leader and follower feel like they won.

How do I teach this? Instead of giving students a firm yes or no to a request, let the child make a new suggestion and allow them time to process and provide a counteroffer. Start off with small tasks and role-playing. This will improve students' problem solving and negotiation skills.

Leaders Have Hobbies

Leaders have hobbies because it's a good way to turn off work or stress, redirect energy, demonstrate responsibility, and ignite creativity.

Why is this important? Hobbies are fulfilling and relaxing, and it's often during those hobbies that leaders come up with the best ideas!

How do I teach this? Some families have hobbies like running, biking, and collectibles. Other individual hobbies are great too, such as painting, baking, and gardening. Encourage students to record a video or do a presentation on their hobby. When students share, you are giving them the opportunity to be leaders in their respective fields, gain confidence, and enhance their presenting and speaking skills in the classroom.

Leaders Know How to Give Recognition

Recognizing the value and talents of the people around you demonstrate that you value and respect your fellow classmates.

Why is this important? By recognizing others, you are creating a positive environment. This is a valuable leadership tool that creates an environment where people are compelled to give their best.

How do I teach this? Some examples of giving recognition can be a handwritten note or an announcement. Children love to create cards and draw pictures. If the student is too small to write a message, have them dictate their message while you write it down. This will help reinforce the relationship between words and letters along with making others feel good.

Leaders Brainstorm

Brainstorming is a process that helps us achieve a goal or fix a problem.

Why is this important? As leaders, brainstorming is extremely important because we do this on a somewhat daily basis. As time and technology change at the speed of light... we need the ability to brainstorm and problem-solve an array of problems.

How do I teach this? Give students the opportunity to change the end of a story during story time in class. For example, the tortoise won the race, but what could the hare have done differently to win? What if there were five bears and only three bowls of porridge? This will also serve as a great brainstorming exercise that students can do with their parents in the car on the way home from school.

Leaders Are Courageous

Courageous people have the ability to take a stand and advocate for themselves or the people they care about.

Why is this important? As leaders, sometimes we stand alone in decision making, advocating, or defending something we believe in. We cannot fight our students' battles but teaching them to be courageous equips them to handle their problems on their own as they get older.

How do I teach this? Have discussions about courage with your class. Ask questions such as, "What does courage look like? Who are some people who demonstrate courage?" Some examples could be political or spiritual individuals in history or the community. There are also many children's books that give great examples, like the children's biographies of Martin Luther King, Jr., and Abraham Lincoln.

Early Life Leadership Infusion

Early Life Leadership Lesson Plan

Leadership Skill of the Day	**What do you want the child to learn?**
Strategies or Teaching Methods Used	**Adult Observation**
Open-Ended Question #1 Q. Why? How? What does that look like?	**Open-Ended Question #2** Q. Why? How? What does that look like?
Strengths of the Lesson	Recommendations for Reteach

<table>
<tr><th>K</th><th>E</th><th>W</th><th>L</th></tr>
<tr>
<td>What do I know about leadership?</td>
<td>What is my leadership experience?</td>
<td>What do I want to know?</td>
<td>What have I learned?</td>
</tr>
</table>

Early Life Leadership Teacher Reflection

» How am I infusing leadership in my students?

» What is the Leadership skill I want the child to learn?

» How did I introduce the skill to the child?

» How did the child respond?

» How did I model the skill to the child?

» Did I use any visual examples?

» How did I reteach the skill?

» What was different than the first time?

» What were some real-life experiences the child could connect the leadership skill too?

How Can I Implement Leadership in My Classroom?

What worked for me was 10-15 minutes in the morning while the kids were eating breakfast. We would have a discussion question of the day, or a student would sign up to present or share something personal. This was an excellent way to make real-life connections.

Leadership Integration:

- Reading about leaders
- Writing about leaders
- Trailblazers in Technology Leadership
- Historical Leadership
- Trailblazers in Science, Technology, Engineering, & Math Leadership

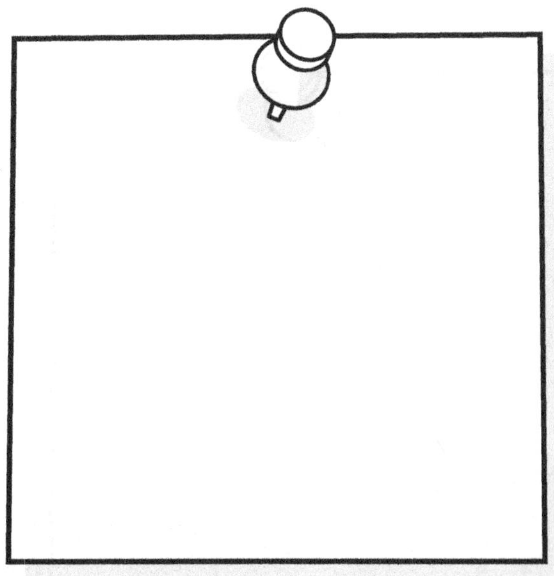

You may want to also try:

- Leadership wall or bulletin board
- Leadership collage posters
- Leadership journals
- Leadership dress-up
- Leadership family tree
- Leadership book of the day or read-aloud
- Leaders in my community
- Global Leadership & Culture

Thinking Cloud Worksheet Instructions

Leadership Question of the Day

There is a misconception that leadership takes a long time to learn. Leadership can be sprinkled into the classroom by posting a "Leadership Question of the Day." Make copies of the Thinking Cloud worksheet from this chapter and have children either draw or write (depending on their grade level) their answers to the leadership question each day. Some children may want to do both.

Leadership Question
of the Day

This is a great opportunity to:

- ask higher-level questions
- incorporate classroom behavior needs
- incorporate specific vocabulary
- increase positive behavior and classroom management

Some question openers that ignite thinking include:

- Why?
- How?
- What does that look like?

10 Leadership Questions for Children

📚 What does leadership look like?	
📚 What is passion, and why is it important to leadership?	

📚 Who are the people who have created things that make the world better? How are they leaders?	
📚 What are some things you love to do? (cooking, dancing, drawing, painting, pottery, wildlife exploration, technology, athletics) Are you a leader in that field?	

📚 How can you take your hobbies or the things you love to do to another level? (books, YouTube or TV show, services offered, companions) How can you use your hobbies to be a better leader?	
📚 What invention can you create to make an impact or difference?	

📚 How do your passions, hobbies, strengths, and creativity make you a better leader?	
📚 How can a leader change lives?	

📚 Who are the people in your life whom you see as leaders, and why?	
📚 What are some problems in the world we have that good leaders could fix?	

Early Life Leadership Grid Instructions

The Early Life Leadership Grid template may be used as:

» an outline for leadership activities

» a journal template (some classrooms have leadership journals)

» a library research template (students may read specific books picked by the adult and the adult can add thought-provoking questions)

Early Life Leadership Grid

<table>
<tr><td>Leadership skill of the day</td><td></td></tr>
<tr><td>Leadership skill defined</td><td></td></tr>
<tr><td>What do I know about this leadership skill?</td><td></td></tr>
<tr><td>Why is this leadership skill important to learn?</td><td></td></tr>
<tr><td>What did I learn about this leadership skill?</td><td></td></tr>
<tr><td>What do I want to learn more about?</td><td></td></tr>
</table>

Early Life Leadership Brainstorming Cards

These cards are great for:

- » using at a leadership center

- » encouraging the brainstorming of leadership ideas for projects, discussions, and essays

- » encouraging students to present on the card they picked

- » using in group or pair discussions

 Who can I help?	 How can I make the world sweeter?	 What would I like to accomplish?
 What do I listen to? Does it help me be a better leader?	 Whose life story have I learned from?	 What is special about my world?

<table>
<tr>
<td>
What do I know about the fine arts? Who are some famous leaders and why?</td>
<td>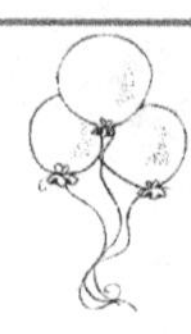
How do I celebrate my life and the lives of others?</td>
<td>
How can I take care of my community and the earth?</td>
</tr>
<tr>
<td>
What does it mean to walk in other people's shoes, and what does it look like?</td>
<td>
I always have energy to________!</td>
<td>
I love being a leader because ________!</td>
</tr>
</table>

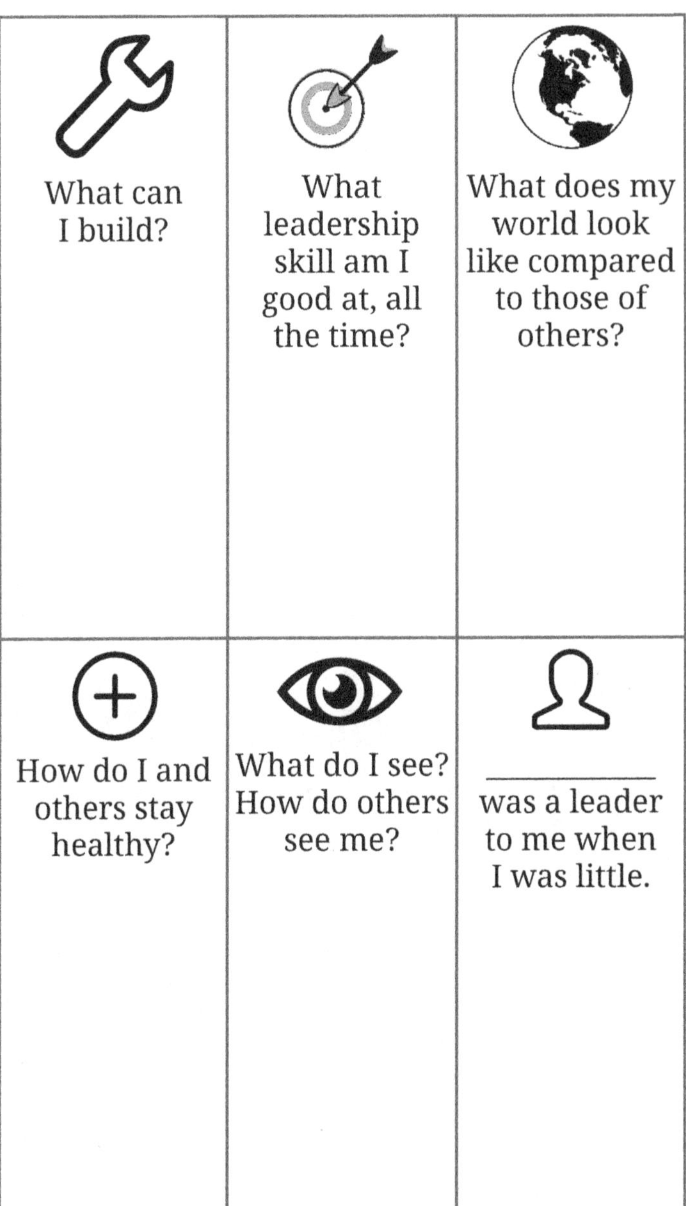

What can
I build?

What
leadership
skill am I
good at, all
the time?

What does my
world look
like compared
to those of
others?

How do I and
others stay
healthy?

What do I see?
How do others
see me?

____
was a leader
to me when
I was little.

What do I do when I have been treated unfairly?

What can I grow?

It's time to_____!

I can teach others how to_____ !

Money can't buy_______.

Animals make the world better because __________!

Leadership Tree

"Growing My Strengths"

Directions: What are some of your leadership strengths? Write one leadership strength in each leaf.

Leader Acrostic Poem

Directions: You can easily write an acrostic poem! Each line of the poem should consist of a word or phrase related to you and your leadership abilities.

L ------------------------------

E ------------------------------

A ------------------------------

D ------------------------------

E ------------------------------

R ------------------------------

Leadership Gallery

Directions: Draw, doodle, or write four things you are proud of in your leadership life!

Early Life Leadership In Action

Directions: On the left side of the circle, note your strengths. On the right, note your weaknesses, and in the overlapping part in the middle, note the leadership skills you are working on. Potentialities are skills that are not quite mastered yet but have the potential to be strengths; these are written in the middle.

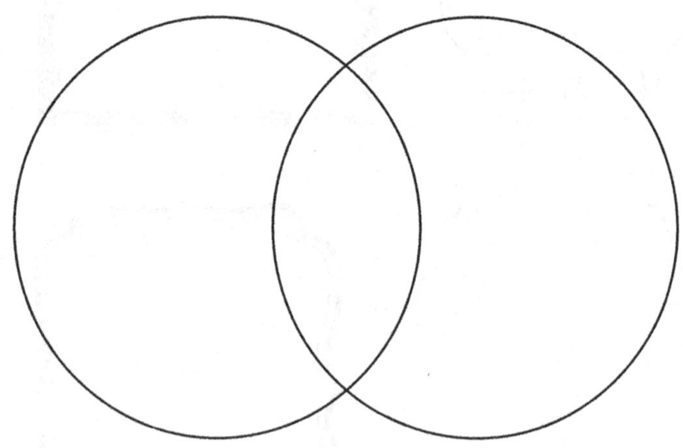

Leadership Shield

Directions: Use the leadership shield to set four leadership goals. Draw or write one leadership goal in each section.

15 Affirmations for Early Life Leaders

1. My words have the power
   to make things better.
2. My family loves me.
3. It makes me feel good to help others.
4. My voice matters.
5. I enjoy being challenged
   because I am strong.
6. I can make mistakes and still be
   loved because no one is perfect.
7. I am a good person who tries to
   consider other people's feelings.
8. I have the power to reach my goals.
9. I deserve to be accepted for my true self.
10. I can make mistakes and
    still reach my goals.
11. I know I need to take time to
    relax and clear my mind.
12. I am confident.
13. I believe in myself.
14. I speak to myself with kindness.
15. I don't compare myself to others because
    we are all different like fingerprints.

Early Life Leadership Positive Praise

1. You are a great leader!
2. I love your ideas!
3. How Creative
4. You're Amazing
5. It's everything I expected!
6. Nice Going
7. How Artistic
8. You are an awesome team leader!
9. Fantastic Work
10. Thumbs Up
11. You're a shining star
12. You are Great!
13. You are a great friend!
14. You are a great remodel!
15. You Make Me Smile
16. You're Unique
17. Your Help Counts!
18. That's Incredible
19. Thank you for your effort!
20. You have good manners!
21. Outstanding
22. You deserve a hug
23. Thank you for being respectful!
24. Phenomenal!

25. You are a hard worker!
26. You're Inspiring
27. What a Great Idea
28. Thank you for being open-minded
29. I knew you had it in you!
    Thank you for trying.
30. You're So Kind
31. You're a Champ
32. What a Genius!
33. I appreciate your help!
34. You are brave!
35. Excellent!
36. You are a great risk-taker! Thank
    you for trying something new.
37. Thanks for Caring
38. Thank you for thinking about
    other people's feelings.
39. Amazing Effort!
40. You are a wonderful listener.

Leadership Skill	The Child's Strengths: The Child's Weakness:
Teach: Reteach:	Activity: Positive Praise : "I Do" ___________________ "We Do" _______________ "You Do" _______________

Early Life Leadership Notes

Leadership Skill	The Child's Strengths:
	The Child's Weakness:
Teach: Reteach:	Activity: Positive Praise : "I Do" ________________ "We Do" ______________ "You Do" ______________

Early Life Leadership Notes

Leadership Skill	The Child's Strengths: The Child's Weakness:
Teach: Reteach:	Activity: Positive Praise : "I Do" ___________________ "We Do" ___________________ "You Do" ___________________

Early Life Leadership Notes

Leadership Skill	The Child's Strengths: The Child's Weakness:
Teach: Reteach:	Activity: Positive Praise : "I Do" _________________ "We Do" _______________ "You Do" ______________

Early Life Leadership Notes

Leadership Skill	The Child's Strengths: The Child's Weakness:
Teach: Reteach:	Activity: Positive Praise : "I Do" _________________ "We Do" _________________ "You Do" _________________

Early Life Leadership Notes

Early Life Leadership in the Classroom Conclusion

We can all agree that we want the children in our lives to be successful. We want our kiddos happy and healthy, but what actions are we taking? Life is already complex, but if we take five minutes a day to do one small tidbit in this book, all the while creating a supportive, friendly environment where children are free to explore who they are as leaders, we can take the children in our lives to the next level.

Early Life Leadership in the Classroom can be effective if we are consistent and may foster self-esteem, autonomy, self-reliance, attainable achievement, and motivation for learning and leading others. I once received an email asking, "why do you say, 'the children in our lives versus students?'" My response was, "because we are all teachers, regardless if we are teachers or not; or parents or not. It is our responsibility as adults to teach every child that crosses our path."

Be blessed friends and please email me if you questions.

Thank you, -CD
christinademara@gmail.com

Also Written by Christina DeMara

My Prayer Book

Peace is Mine
The Forgiveness Journal

I'm Not Broken
The Power of Prayer, Scripture, and Interactive Journaling

How God Saved Me
My Mother's Memoirs on Abuse, Depression & Overeating

The I Am Journal
A Soul-Searching Journal for Creative Women of God

Isaiah 43:2
40 Days of Scriptures, Reflection, and Journaling for the Lent Season

Meaningful Books & Resources

Meaningful Leadership
How to Build Indestructible Relationships with Your Team Members Through Intentionality and Faith

Meaningful Leadership Journal

Meaningful Leadership Prayer Journal

Meaningful Teacher Leadership
Reflection, Refinement, and Student Achievement

Meaningful Writing & Self-Publishing
Your Guide to Igniting Your Pen, Faith, Creativity & Entrepreneurship

About the Author

Christina DeMara is passionate about her relationship with God, Jesus, and the Holy Spirit. Christina loves writing books, worship music, learning, leading, teaching, and living life significantly. She is the creative mind behind the coined leadership theories titled *Early Life Leadership Infusion* and *Meaningful Leadership*. She holds three master's degrees from the University of Texas: one in Special Education, one in Educational Administration and Leadership, and one in Curriculum and Instruction. She later studied business and leadership extensively for six years through Our Lady of the Lake University in San Antonio, Texas. Christina is best known for the creative concepts found in *Early Life Leadership in Children, Early Life Leadership in Girls Workbook*, and her Christian book titled *I'm Not Broken, The Power of Prayer, Scripture, and Interactive Journaling*.

BONUS!

Free Copy of the Meaningful Teacher Leadership Grid

****Available at Barnes & Noble and Amazon****

Memo- rization Icon	"OW" Leadership Reflection	Internalization What does that look like? Draw a picture or symbol.	What do I need to do to nurture this area?
	KNOW: What do I know about leadership?		
	GLOW: What are my leadership qualities that glow? How do I stand out?		
	SHOW: What do I show others? How do others perceive me?		
	GROW: How am I growing as a leader? What am I doing to improve my leadership skills?		

Memo-rization Icon	"OW" Leadership Reflection	Internalization What does that look like? Draw a picture or symbol.	What do I need to do to nurture this area?
	SNOW: What is cold in my leadership life that requires attention?		
	BOWL: What is in my bowl? What leadership resources do I have?		
	MOW: What is mowing me down and stopping me from moving to the next level of leadership greatness?		

Memo-rization Icon	"OW" Leadership Reflection	Internalization What does that look like? Draw a picture or symbol.	What do I need to do to nurture this area?
	FLOW: What is flowing smoothly? What are the things going good in the leadership aspect of my life?		
	TOW: What am I towing that may be slowing me down from reaching my full leadership potential?		
	BOW: What am I ready to launch forward?		

Memorization Icon	"OW" Leadership Reflection	Internalization What does that look like? Draw a picture or symbol.	What do I need to do to nurture this area?
	LOW: What is an area of weakness I need to work on?		
	SOW: What am I working on? Remember, you reap what you sow!		
	ROW: What am I rowing towards? Am I going in the right direction?		
	OWE: Who do I owe for mentoring me? What am I taking away from my mentors?		

Please Connect with Christina!

She would love to hear from you!

Christina has two Facebook groups called

I Love Reading & Writing

and

I Love Leadership

for her readers.

You are welcome to join!

Bless This Book!

If you enjoyed this book or any other of Christina's books, your honest review is greatly appreciated! Reviews help the author's books be seen by others and help the writer qualify for different book promotions.

Your Time and Review is Appreciated!

Questions?

ChristinaDeMara.com

EarlyLifeLeadership.com

christinademara@gmail.com

Bibliography

Ackerman, D., & Barnett, W. (2005). Prepared for Kindergarten: What Does "Readiness" Mean? Preschool Policy Brief for the National Institute for Early Education Research, 13-13.

Addison, L., Oliver, A. I., & Cooper, C. R. (1987). Developing leadership potential in gifted children and youth. Reston, VA: ERIC Clearinghouse on Handicapped and Gifted Children.

Andersen, L. (2011). The effects of formal leadership-lessons on the emergence of positive social-leadership skills of pre-kindergarten students.

Asendorpf, J. B., & Van Aken, M. A. G. (2002). Validity of big five personality judgments in childhood: A 9-year longitudinal study; 17: 1-17 (2003).

Ayman, R., & Korabik, K. (2010). Leadership: Why gender and culture matter. American Psychologist, 65(3), 157.

Berkowitz, M. (2009). Character education and gifted children. High Ability Studies, 20(2), 131-142.

Bisland, A. (January 01, 2004). Developing Leadership Skills in Young Gifted Students. The Gifted Child Today, 27, 24-31.

Bohlin, L. C. (2000). Determinants of young children's leadership and dominance strategies during play. (9993607, Indiana University). ProQuest Dissertations and Theses. 139-139 p.

Boseovski, J. J., Shallwani, S., & Lee, K. (2009). It's all good: Children's personality attributions after repeated success and failure in peer and computer interactions. British Journal of Developmental Psychology, 27(4), 783-797.

Brenner, S. C. (1991). Leadership characteristics in young children as perceived by caregivers in a child care setting. Philadelphia, Pa.

Burchinal, M., Howes, C., Pianta, R., Bryant, D., Early, D., Clifford, R., & Barbarin, O. (2008). Predicting child outcomes at the end of kindergarten from the quality of pre-kindergarten teacher-child interactions and instruction. Applied Developmental Science, 12(3), 140-153.

Campbell, R. (2007, January 1). Leadership: Getting It Done. Retrieved September 6, 2014, from http://web.missouri.edu/~campbellr/Leadership/chapter4.htm

Carver, C. L. (2012). Developing Leadership Content Knowledge during School Leader Preparation. International Journal of Educational Leadership Preparation, 7(3)l.

Caspi, A., Harrington, H., Milne, B., Amell, J. W., Theodore, R. F., & Moffitt, T. E. (2003). Children's behavioral styles at age 3 are linked to their adult personality traits at age 26. Journal of Personality, 71(4), 495 - 513.

Castillo, C. T. (2001). The effects of a dual-language education program on student achievement and development of leadership abilities. (Order No. 3022340, Our Lady of the Lake University). ProQuest Dissertations and Theses, 77-77 p. Retrieved from http://search.proquest.com/docview/251479399?accountid=7058. (251479399). Centers for Disease Control and Prevention.

Charlesworth, R. (1987). Understanding child development. (2nd ed.). Albany, New York: Delmar Publishers Inc.

Chetty, R., Friedman, J. N., Hilger, N., Saenz, E., Schanzenbach, D. W., & Yagan, D. (2010, November 1). $320,000 Kindergarten Teachers. Kappan, 22-25.

Chickering, A. & Gamson Z. 1987, "Seven principles for good practice in undergraduate education," Reprinted by Honolulu Community College, National Learning Infrastructure Initiative, 2003, Mapping the Learning Space: Design Implications, Educause, viewed 23 March 2004

Clotfelter, Charles T. & Ladd, Helen F. & Vigdor, Jacob L., 2007. "Teacher credentials and student achievement: Longitudinal analysis with student fixed effects," Economics of Education Review, Elsevier, vol. 26(6), pages 673-682, December

Colker, L. J. Twelve Characteristics of Early Childhood Teachers. Beyond the Journal: Young Children on the Web, 1-6.

Cummins, J. (2000). Language, power, and pedagogy bilingual children in the crossfire. Clevedon, England: Multilingual Matters

Dhuey, E., & Lipscomb, S. (2006). What Makes a Leader? Relative Age and High School Leadership. Economics of Education Review, 27(2), 173-183.

Do Kindergarten Teachers Make a Difference?. (2010, August 2).]

Eagly Johannesen-Schmidh and van Engen (2003) Transformational, transactional, and laissez-faire leadership styles: A meta-analysis comparing women and men. Psychological Bulletin, 129(4), 569-591.

Educational Testing Service (2012). Relationships between Big Five and Academic and Workforce Outcomes.]

Ehrler, D. J., Evans, J. G. and McGhee, R. L. (1999), Extending Big-Five theory into childhood: A preliminary investigation into the relationship between Big-Five personality traits and behavior problems in children. Psychol. Schs., 36: 451–458.

Fox, Deborah Lee, "Teachers' Perceptions of Leadership in Young Children" (2012). University of New Orleans Theses and Dissertations. Paper 1546.

French, D. C., & Stright, A. L. (1991). Emergent leadership in children's small groups. Small Group Research, 22(2), 187-199.

French, D. C., Waas, G. A., Stright, A. L., & Baker, J. A. (1986). Leadership asymmetries in mixed-age children's groups. Child Development, 1277-1283.

Fu, V. R. (1979). Preschool leadership-followership behaviors. Child Study Journal, 9(2), 133-140.

Fu, V. R. (1970). The development of a nursery school leadership observation schedule and a nursery school leadership rating scale.

Fukada, H., Fukada, S., & Hicks, J. (1997). The relationship between leadership and sociometric status among preschool children. The Journal of Genetic Psychology, 158(4), 481-486.

Genesee, F., & Paradis, J. (2004). Dual language development and disorders: A handbook on bilingualism and second language learning. Baltimore, Maryland: Paul H. Brookes Publishing.

Goldberg, L. R. (1993). The structure of phenotypic personality traits. American psychologist, 48(1), 26.

Gravetter, F., & Wallnau, L. (2009). Statistics for the behavioral sciences (8th ed.). Belmont, CA: Wadsworth.

Gullo, D. F., Heroman, C., & Copple, C., (2002). Teaching and Learning in the Kindergarten Year. K Today.

Guthrie, K., Jones, T., Hu, S., & Osteen, L. (2013). Cultivating leader identity and capacity in students from diverse backgrounds. Hoboken, NJ: Wiley Periodicals.

Hahn, E., Gottschling, J., & Spinath, F. M. (June 01, 2012). Short measurements of personality - Validity, and reliability of the GSOEP Big Five Inventory (BFI-S). Journal of Research in Personality, 46, 3, 355-359.

Hampson SE, Goldberg LR.; J Pers Soc Psychol. 2006 Oct;91(4):763-79.

Hampson SE, Goldberg LR, Vogt TM, Dubanoski JP., Health Psychol. 2006 Jan;25(1):57-64. PMID: 16448298

Henry, M. (1998). The Manager's Job: Folklore and Fact. In Harvard Business Review on Leadership. Boston, Mass.: Harvard Business School Publishing.

Hensel, N. H. (1991). Social leadership skills in young children. Roeper Review, 14(1), 4.

Hess, L. (2010). Student leadership education in elementary classroom. San Rafael, Calif: Dominican University of California.

Honigsfeld, A., & Cohan, A. (2012). Breaking the Mold of Education for Culturally and Linguistically Diverse Students. Lanham, ML: Roman & Littlefield Education.

Howard, P., & Howard, J. (2001). The owner's manual for personality at work: How the big five personality traits affect performance, communication, teamwork, leadership, and sales. Marietta, GA: Bard Press.

Irby, B. J., & Lara-Alecio, R. (1996). Attributes of Hispanic Gifted Bilingual Students as Perceived by Bilingual Educators in Texas. SABE Journal, 11, 120-143.

Kirnon, S. N., & Pepperdine University. (2008). Inspiring citizenship and leadership: Youth citizenship seminar.

John, O. P., Naumann, L. P., & Soto, C. J. (2008). Paradigm Shift to the Integrative Big-Five Trait Taxonomy: History, Measurement, and Conceptual Issues. In O. P. John, R. W. Robins, & L. A. Pervin (Eds.), Handbook of personality: Theory and research (pp. 114-158). New York, NY: Guilford Press.

Judge, Timothy A.; Bono, Joyce E.; Ilies, Remus; Gerhardt, Megan W. Journal of Applied Psychology, Vol 87(4), Aug 2002, 765-780. doi: 10.1037/0021-9010.87.4.765

Judkins Jr., P. A. Certain criteria lead toward leadership. Operations and Planning Rural Health Association, Farming, Maine.

Karschney, K. J. (2003). Structured intergenerational dialogue: A multiple case study of eleven children in a leadership workshop. (Order No. 3106567, Gonzaga University). ProQuest Dissertations and Theses, 261-261 p. http://search.proquest.com/docview/305278835?accountid=7058. (305278835).

Lamon, C. C., & Valdosta State University. (2005). The impact of the Georgia Pre-K Program on the achievement gap between at-risk and not-at-risk students for kindergarten readiness as measured by teacher perception and student assessments.

Lee, Y., & Recchia, S. L. (2008). "Who's the Boss?" Young Children's Power and Influence in an Early Childhood Classroom. Early Childhood Research & Practice, 10(1).

Lee, P., Lan, W., Wang, C., & Chiu, H. (2008). Helping Young Children to Delay Gratification. Early Childhood Education Journal, 35(6), 557-564.

Lester, J. E. (2002) Does Your Child Have Leadership Ability?. Ohio Leadership Institute.

Li, Y., Anderson, R. C., Nguyen-Jahiel, K., Dong, T., Archodidou, A., Kim, I. H., & Miller, B. (2007). Emergent leadership in children's discussion groups. Cognition and Instruction, 25(1), 1-2.

Lieberman, L. J., Arndt, K., & Daggett, S. (2007). Promoting leadership in physical education and recreation. Journal of Physical Education, Recreation & Dance, 78(3), 46-50.

MacLure, M., Jones, L., Holmes, R., & MacRae, C. (2012). Becoming a Problem: Behavior and Reputation in the Early Years Classroom. British Educational Research Journal, 38(3), 447-471.

Manley, M., & Northeastern University (Boston, Mass.). (2013). A mixed methods study on leadership, communication, cooperation, and collaboration in children enrolled in the learning leadership academy.

Markey, P. M., Markey, C. N., & Tinsley, B. J. (2004). Children's behavioral manifestations of the five-factor model of personality. Personality and Social Psychology Bulletin, 30(4), 423-432.

Mawson, B. (2011). Children's Leadership Strategies in Early Childhood. Journal of Research in Childhood Education, 25(4), 327-338.

Maynard, T., & Nigel, T. (2004). An introduction to early childhood studies. Thousand Oaks, California: Sage Publications Ltd.

Meriweather, S., & Karnes, F. A. (1989). Parents' Views on Leadership. Gifted Child Today (GCT), 12(1), 55-59.

Minnesota Early Childhood Teacher Educators. (1986). Kindergarten excellence: Knowledge and competencies of kindergarten teachers. St. Paul, MN: Minnesota Dept. of Education.

Murray, J., Theakston, A., & Wells, A. (2016). Can the attention training technique turn one marshmallow into two? Improving children's ability to delay gratification. Behavior Research and Therapy, 77, 34-39. doi:10.1016/j.brat.2015.11.009

National Society for the Gifted and Talented (2012). Giftedness defined - what is gifted & talented?.

Nelson, A. E. (January 01, 2010). In focus youth leadership—Stepping in early to grow great leaders. Leadership in Action, 29, 6, 20-24.

New Jersey Department of Education. (1999) Have Your Heard? The Truth About Kindergarten. A Guide to Understanding Kindergarten.

Olivero, J. L.; Leading leaders. Nueva Learning Center.

Piaget, J. (1952). The origins of intelligence in children (Vol. 8, No. 5, p. 18). New York: International Universities Press.

Pandya, A. A., & Jogsan, Y. A. (2013). Personality and Locus of Control among School Children. Educational Research and Reviews, 8(22), 2193-2196.

Parmer, L. (2012). The relationship between personality and leadership in adolescents. (Order No. 3535621, Our Lady of the Lake University). ProQuest Dissertations and Theses, 201. Retrieved from http://search.proquest.com/docview/1283388608?accountid=7058. (1283388608).

Parten, M. B. (1933). Leadership among preschool children. The Journal of Abnormal and Social Psychology, 27(4), 430.

Prepared for Kindergarten: What Does "Readiness" Mean? Preschool Policy Brief for the National Institute for Early Education Research, 13-13.

Pramling Samuelsson, I., & Kaga, Y. (2008). The contribution of early childhood education to a sustainable society. Paris, UNESCO.

Lord, Robert G.; de Vader, Christy L.; Alliger, George M. Journal of Applied Psychology, Vol 71(3), Aug 1986, 402-410.

Leadership giftedness in preschool children. Roeper Review, 4, 3, 26-28.

Rios, L. A. (2010). The relationship between emerging leadership behavior in children and their academic performance. Our Lady of the Lake University).

Rogelberg, S. G. (Ed.). (2006). Encyclopedia of industrial and organizational psychology. Sage Publications.

Rushton, J. (1966). The relationship between personality characteristics and scholastics success in eleven-year-old children. The British Journal of Educational Psychology, 36(The University of Manchester), 178-183.

Russell, B., Londhe, R., & Britner, P. (2013). Parental Contributions to the Delay of Gratification in Preschool-aged Children. Journal of Child & Family Studies, 22(4), 471-478. doi:10.1007/s10826-012-9599-8

Ryan, K., & Cooper, J. (2010). Kaleidoscope: Contemporary and classic readings in education (12th ed.). Belmont, Calif.: Wadsworth Cengage Learning.

Scharf, M., & Mayseless, O. (2009). Socioemotional Characteristics of Elementary School Children Identified as Exhibiting Social Leadership Qualities. Journal of Genetic Psychology, 170(1), 73-94.

Schoenfeldt, K. R. (2012). Kindergarten program type as a predictor for reading achievement in third grade. (Doctoral dissertation), Available from ProQuest Dissertations & Theses.

Serafin, A. G. (1992). Charismatic Behaviors and Traits of Future Educational Leaders.

Shaunessy, E., & Karnes, F. A. (2004). Instruments for Measuring Leadership in Children and Youth. Gifted Child Today, 27(1), 42-47.

Shipley, G. L. (1998). Early childhood educators' perceptions of kindergarten readiness in a southern Ohio school district: Implications for educational leadership.

Short, D., & Echevarria, J. (2005). Teacher Skill to Support English Language Learners. The Best of Educational Leadership 2004-2005, 62, 8-13.

Silverman, L. K. (2000). Counseling the gifted and talented. (1 ed.). Denver, CO: Love Publishing Company.

Soffler, A. A. (2011). What is the Nature of Children's Leadership in Early Childhood Educational Settings? A Grounded Theory. Fort Collins, Co.: Colorado State University.

Srivastava, S. (2015). Measuring the Big Five Personality Factors. Retrieved March 18, 2015.

Stark, P. (Ed.). (2014, July 1). Glossary of Statistical Terms. Retrieved from http://www.stat.berkeley.edu/~stark/SticiGui/Text/gloss.htm#categorical

Texas English Language Learners Portal. (2012). Retrieved December 27, 2015.

The development of markers for the Big-Five factor structure. Goldberg, Lewis R. Psychological Assessment, Vol 4(1), Mar 1992, 26-42.

Trawick-Smith, J. (1988). "Let's say you're the baby, OK?" Play leadership and following behavior of young children. Young Children.

Villagomez, E. T. (2007). An inductive analysis of the self-perceptions of young children related to leadership as a construct. Our Lady of the Lake University). ProQuest Dissertations and Theses, http://search.proquest.com/docview/304717742?accountid=7058

Vygotsky, L. S. (1967). Play and its role in the mental development of the child. Journal of Russian and East European Psychology, 5(3), 6-18.

Wells, C. (1986). The meaning makers: Children learning language and using language to learn (1st ed.). Portsmouth, N.H.: Heinemann.

2013 Social Enterprise Conference, Columbia Business School. (2013, January 1). Do Kindergarten Teachers Make a Difference?. Retrieved, from http://blog.columbiasocialenterprise.org/

Made in the USA
Monee, IL
07 July 2026

56546638R00066